HOW ANIMALS Hide

By Robert M. McClung

Thorn Bug

BOOKS FOR YOUNG EXPLORERS
NATIONAL GEOGRAPHIC SOCIETY

Library of Congress Catalog Number 73-7112 Standard Book Number 87044-144-2

When you play
hide-and-seek,
how do you hide?
Sometimes you duck
behind a tree, or
crawl under a bush.

You hide for fun.
But animals hide
to escape enemies
or to catch something
to eat. This ocelot
can creep up on its prey
without being seen,
because its spotted coat
helps it to hide.
The spots look like
patches of sunlight
on leaves in the jungle.

For a guide to help find the animals
hidden by camouflage, turn to page 40.

But the prey may be hiding too, and perhaps it will escape. A lioness doesn't see a baby gazelle lying in the tall grass. A fawn curls up and waits for its mother to return. It keeps very still, hardly twitching an ear. Its spotted coat blends with the leaves of the forest floor. A hungry bobcat or other enemy would have a hard time seeing it.

White-tailed Fawn

Lioness and Thomson's Gazelle (left)

Some Arctic animals have white coats to match the ice and snow of their northern homes. White fur helps to hide the polar bear. Maybe it can sneak up on a seal. A white coat also helps to hide the baby harp seal and the Arctic fox.

Polar Bear and Cub

Harp Seal Pup

Arctic Fox

Willow Ptarmigan

This bird and hare
change their colors
with the seasons.
During the winter
they are snowy white.

When springtime comes,
they begin to shed their
white coats. Can you see
why this hare is also
called a snowshoe hare?

Varying Hare

As the sun melts the snow from the ground,
the hare grows a new brown coat
for summer, and the bird grows a new set
of spotted brown feathers that match the earth.
Do you see the chick on its mother's back?

Green Tree Frog

The green tree frog hides among green leaves.
So does the poisonous tree snake.
The yellow spider is hard to see as it waits on the
flower to catch flies. Lots of animals
have colors that match the places they live.

Crab Spider

Green Tree Viper

Golden Plovers (above and below)

Woodcock

Whippoorwill

Many birds that nest on the ground have feathers
with patterns that make them hard to see. The eggs of these birds
may also have colors and patterns that help to hide them.
How many golden plover eggs and chicks do you see?
Will enemies find the woodcock and whippoorwill?

Minnow

A big scorpionfish lies on the bottom of the sea, waiting for food. It appears to be part of the rocks and seaweed. The little minnow in the shallow pool is hard to see against the pebbles. A white spider is almost invisible as it moves across the desert.

Running Spider

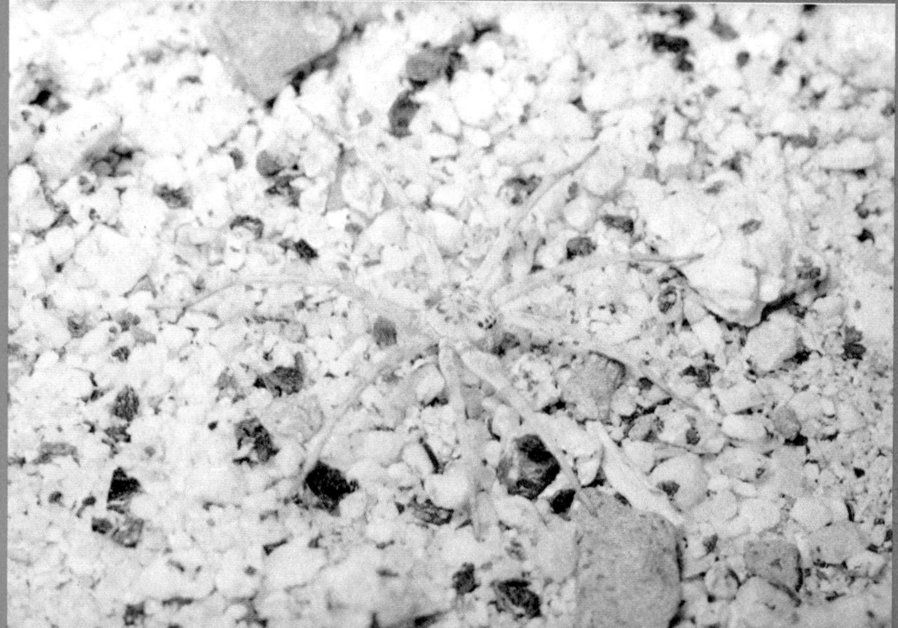

How many horned lizards can you find in the picture? The color, the pattern, and the spiny, flat shape of these reptiles make them very hard to see. As long as the jack rabbit sits still, a hungry fox may not see it.

White-tailed Jack Rabbit

Desert Viper (above) and Eastern Copperhead (right)

It takes sharp eyes to see these snakes.
The poisonous copperhead blends
with the leaves of the forest floor.
The pale desert viper almost disappears
on the ground of its dry homeland.
The adder hides another way.
It buries itself in the sand.
Will other animals be able to see it?

Desert Sidewinding Adder

The peacock flounder seems to be part of the sea. This strange-looking flatfish can change its spots and colors to match the scenery on the ocean floor.

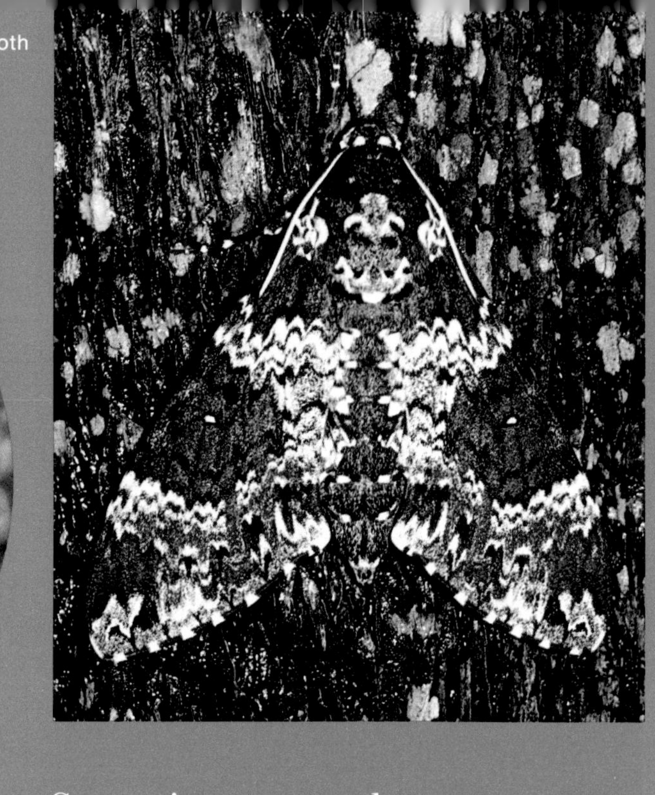

Hawk Moth

Tortoiseshell Butterfly

Some insects and
other animals look like
tree bark. It is hard
to see the butterfly
and moth as they rest
on a tree trunk.
The gecko matches a branch,
and so does the katydid.
A screech owl sits
straight and tall
against a trunk. It seems
to be part of the tree.

Leaf-tailed Gecko

Lichen Katydid

A bittern lifts its head high. In this position it blends with reeds in the swamp. Other animals also hide by taking positions that make them look like things around them.

American Bittern

A trumpetfish stands on its head as it hunts for food among branches of soft coral. An African grasshopper looks like a blade of grass as it perches on a stem.

Grasshopper

Trumpetfish

Measuring Worm

Caterpillars of the Hairstreak Butterfly

Euthalia Caterpillar

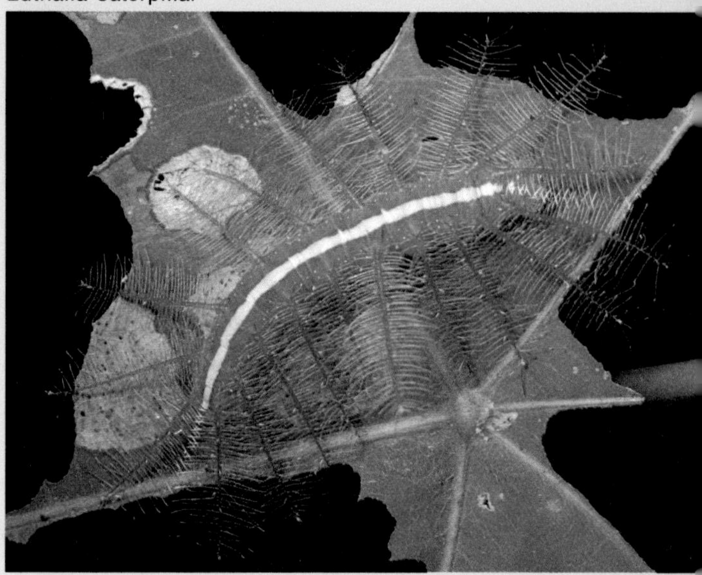

Are they twigs? Are they leaves?
No – they are caterpillars.
The measuring worm looks like
a broken twig. Four green caterpillars
look like they are part of a cypress tree.
With lots of thin, lacy spines and
a stripe down its back another caterpillar
can almost disappear on a leaf.

These insects are mantids. They hunt other insects for food. Some mantids look like leaves. Other mantids look like bark, or stems, or thorny little twigs.

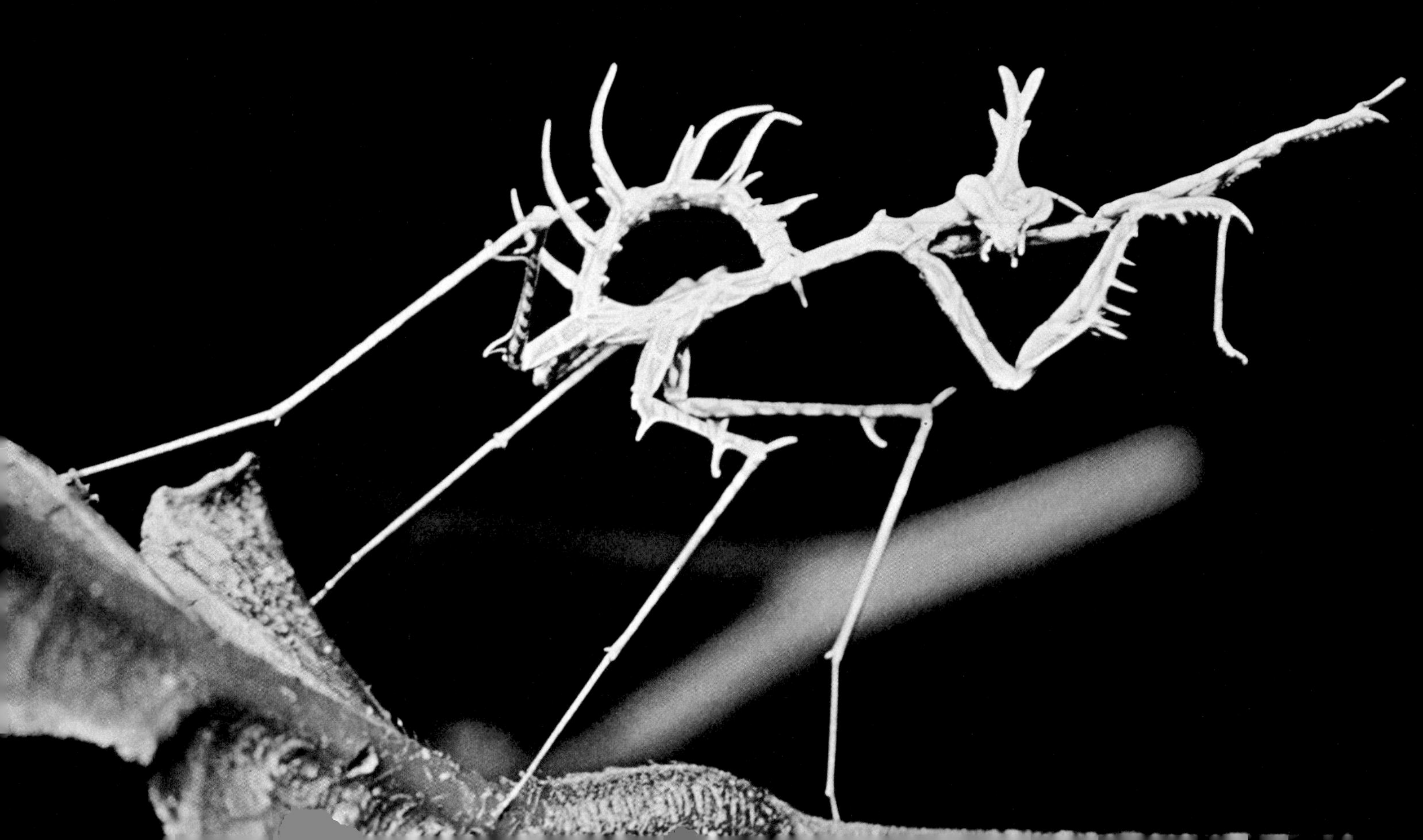

A pink and white flower mantid seems to be part of a blossom.
It perches on an orchid and waits to catch insects.
Its strange shape and colors help it trap its prey and also help the mantid to hide from hungry birds and other animals.

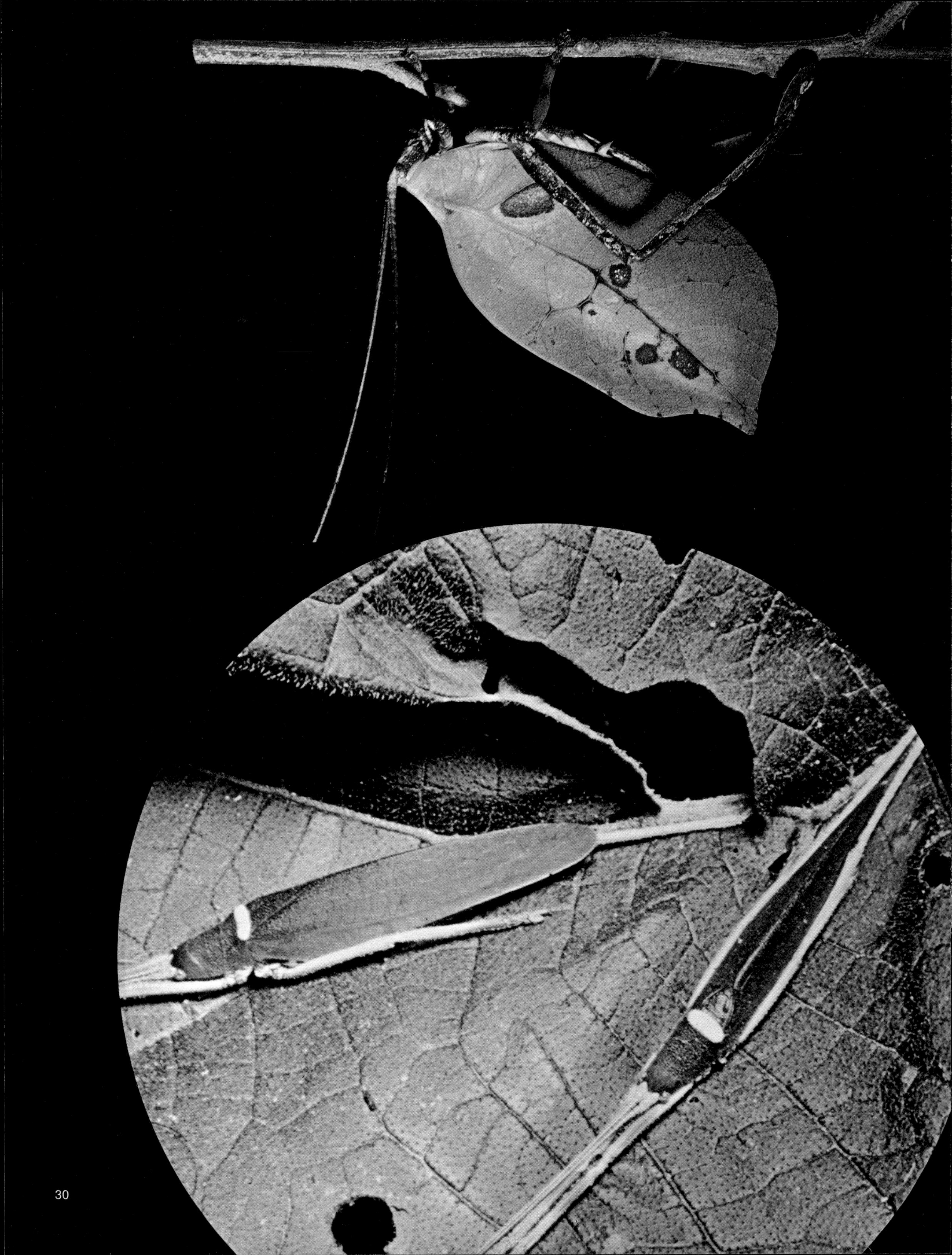

Like mantids, many katydids are protected because they look like something else. Most katydids feed on leaves and spend their lives among them. By looking like leaves, these katydids hide from birds and lizards that like to eat them.

Yellow Jacket

Flower Fly

Birds learn to fear the yellow jacket. It can sting. Its colors and pattern warn birds to keep away. The fly imitates the yellow jacket and fools enemies into leaving it alone. The viceroy butterfly has the same trick. It is tasty, but it imitates the pattern of the bad-tasting monarch butterflies.

Viceroy Butterfly

Monarch Butterflies

Caterpillar of a Noctuid Moth

Io Moth

Fulgorid Bug

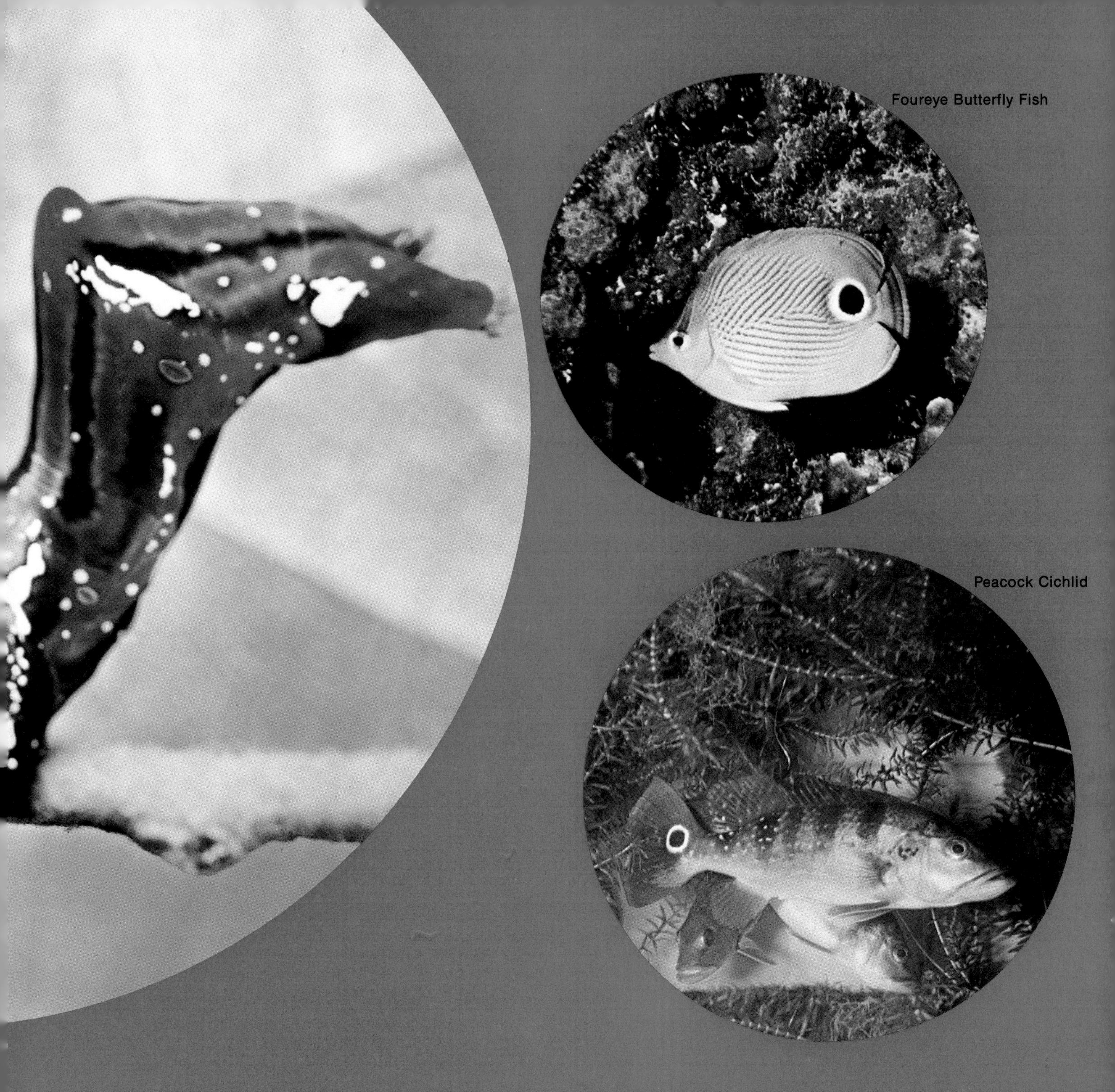

Foureye Butterfly Fish

Peacock Cichlid

Some creatures have spots that look like eyes but are not eyes at all. The caterpillar and moth may scare their enemies with such eyespots. The bug and the two fishes confuse their enemies with eyespots near their tails. It is hard to tell which end is the front and which is the back. If enemies attack the tail, the fish or bug has an extra second to get away.

Sponge Crab

Caddis Fly Larva

The sponge crab holds
a live sponge on its back
with its hind legs. Covered
in this way, the crab is
hard to see. The caddis worm
builds a home from pieces
of leaves and twigs.
Will a fish find it?

Caterpillar of the Blotched Emerald Moth

Bagworm

Decorator Crab

The caterpillar hides by putting bits of leaves on its back. The bagworm makes a bag of leaves. The decorator crab makes a costume of sea plants and animals. It looks like a mossy rock in the sea.

Going, going, gone. An octopus
disappears into a conch shell.
Octopuses find homes in safe places.
They live in the empty homes
of other animals, in undersea caves,
or between rocks. An enemy would have
a hard time getting this little octopus.

How many animals can you think of
that hide in shells? Can you name
animals that make their own shelters?
How many animals can you think of
that are often hidden by their color?
If you look closely, you can see
for yourself how animals hide.

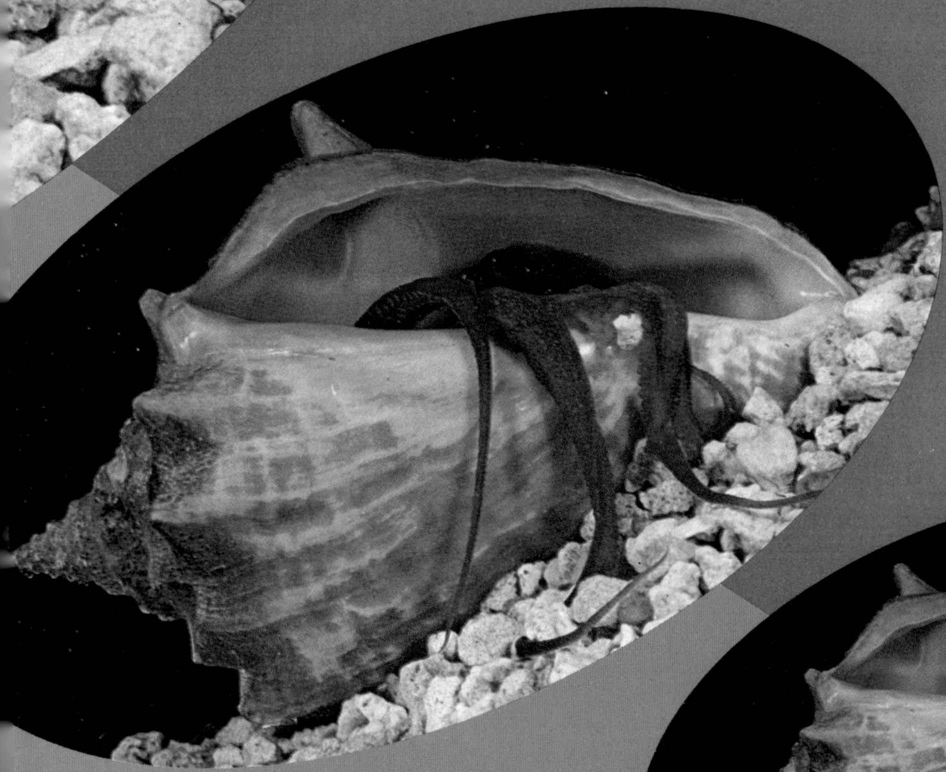

Prepared by the Special Publications Division of the National Geographic Society
Melvin M. Payne, President; Melville Bell Grosvenor, Editor-in-Chief; Gilbert M. Grosvenor, Editor.

Illustrations Credits

James H. Carmichael, Jr. (1), Photo Researchers, Inc. (22 top right); James Holland (2-3); Alan Root (4); Leonard Lee Rue III, National Audubon Society (5); Jack W. Lentfer (6-7 top); Fred Bruemmer (7 bottom left); Joe Rychetnik, Photo Researchers, Inc. (7 bottom right); Charlie Ott, National Audubon Society (8 top left, 9 bottom right), Photo Researchers, Inc. (8 bottom left); Jen and Des Bartlett (8-9 top, 9 top right, 12 top and center); © Tom McHugh, 1972, Photo Researchers, Inc. (8-9 bottom, 37 bottom); Kay and Stanley Breeden (10); Edward S. Ross (11 top and bottom, 15 top and bottom, 18 top, 22 bottom, 25 right, 26-27, 27 right, 28 top right, lower right and bottom, 29, 30-31 all, 32 top and lower, 34-35 top, 34 bottom, 35 center right, 37 top right); © Arthur Butler, Natural History Photographic Agency (12 bottom); Allan Cruickshank, National Audubon Society (13); Walter A. Starck II (14-15, 20-21, 24-25 center); Otha C. Spencer (16-17); C. Allan Morgan (17); Anthony Bannister, Natural History Photographic Agency (18 bottom, 28 top left and right center); Alvin E. Staffan, Photo Researchers, Inc. (18-19); G. E. Hyde, Natural History Photographic Agency (22 top left, 26 left); Alan Root/Tierbilder, Frankfurt/Main (22 center); David Mohrhardt, National Audubon Society (23); Virginia Welch, Photo Researchers, Inc. (24 left); © Ken Brate, 1972, Photo Researchers, Inc. (33 right); Louis Quitt, Photo Researchers, Inc. (34 left); Jerry Greenberg (35 top right); Robert C. Hermes, National Audubon Society (36 top); Stephen Dalton, Natural History Photographic Agency (36 bottom); L. Hugh Newman, Natural History Photographic Agency (37 top left). National Geographic Staff Photographers James P. Blair (33 left); Robert F. Sisson (38-39).

Cover Photograph: Stan Wayman, Photo Researchers, Inc.

The Guide: Maryalyce Reed

A Guide to Animals that Hide

Figures in color reveal the animals hidden by camouflage.

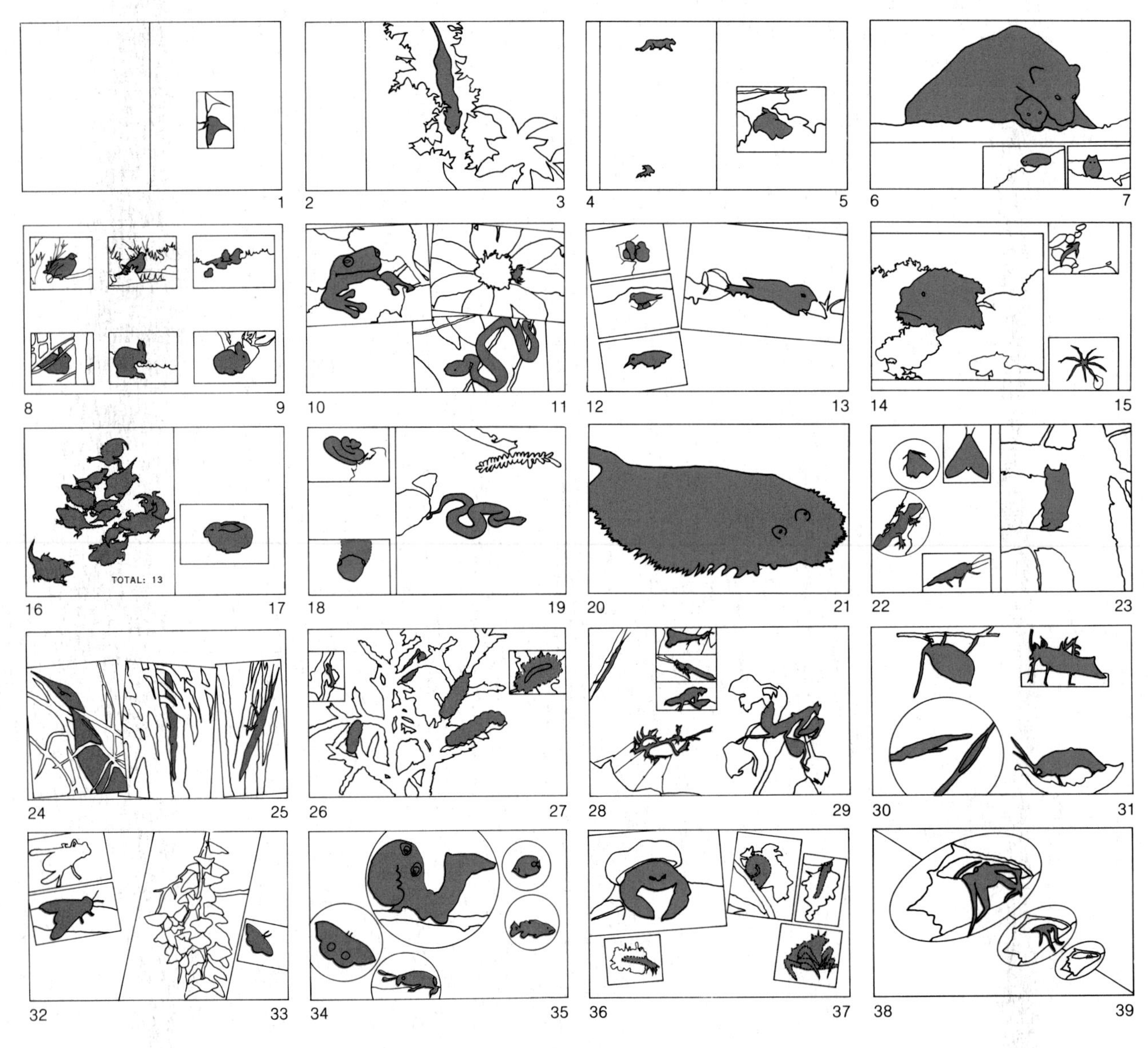